28 Days of Black History: Unsung Heroes

By Marsha Davenport and Allison Dearstyne

For the generations before us who forged ahead with strength and perseverance to accomplish great things. For the generations after us; may you grow up to be as courageous as the people in this book.

Table of Contents

Day 1 - Carter G. Woodson
Day 2 - Mo'Ne Davis
Day 3 - Charlotte E. Ray
Day 4 - Josephine St. Pierre Ruffin
Day 5 - Henry "Box" Brown
Day 6 - William Henry Cling
Day 7 - Matthew Henson
Day 8 - Susie King Taylor
Day 9 - Alexander Miles
Day 10 - George Washington Bush
Day 11 - Daniel Hale Williams
Day 12 - Elizabeth Taylor Greenfield
Day 13 - Benjamin Banneker
Day 14 - Annie Malone
Day 15 - Jan Ernst Matzeliger
Day 16 - Sophia Danenberg
Day 17 - James McCune Smith
Day 18 - Emma Azalia Smith Hackley
Day 19 - Clara Brown
Day 20 - Warren Shadd
Day 21 - Elizabeth Jennings Graham
Day 22 - Charlotte Forten
Day 23 - William Carney
Day 24 - Norbert Rillieux
Day 25 - Harriet Powers
Day 26 - George Speck
Day 27 - Ernest Green
Day 28 - Charlotte Hawkins Brown
Day 29 - Bonus Day

Terms to Know

Abolitionist - someone who wants to put an end to slavery

Activist - someone who works to make changes politically or socially

Apprentice - someone who is learning a trade from a skilled employer, having agreed to work for a period of time at low wages

Civil Rights - the basic rights of all citizens to be treated equally. Historically, the "Civil Rights Movement" referred to efforts toward achieving true equality for Black Americans in all areas of daily living in society.

Civil War - a war between people in the same country. Between 1861 and 1865, there was a Civil War in the United States. The Union Army in the North defeated the Confederate Army in South, and slavery became illegal when the Civil War ended.

Colored or **Negro** - In the 1800s and 1900s these terms were widely used as other words for Black people. These terms appear in this book because some organizations had, and still have, these words in their title. Otherwise, these terms are inappropriate to use.

Discrimination - the unfair treatment of different categories of people

Integration - Bringing people together as equals in society. In 1954, the Supreme Court Case Brown vs. Board of Education made segregation illegal, and called for fair treatment of all races.

Jim Crow Laws - state and local laws that enforced segregation and unfair treatment of Black Americans in the Southern United States. These laws were enforced until 1965.

NAACP - the National Association for the Advancement of Colored People, founded in 1909 to fight segregation and work for the betterment of Black Americans. This organization remains to this day.

Patent - a license issued by the government to give people the exclusive right to make and sell their own inventions

Philanthropist - someone who helps support good causes, especially by donating a lot of money

Prejudice - dislike and hostility that is based on unfounded opinions, not facts

Racism - Prejudice against someone of a different race based on the belief that someone else's own race is superior

Segregation - the separation of different racial groups. In 1892 a Supreme Court Case, Plessy vs. Ferguson, made this legal until the Supreme Court overturned their decision in 1954.

Suffrage - the right to vote

Underground Railroad - a network of secret routes and safe houses where abolitionists helped slaves escape to freedom in Northern states

Day 1 - Carter G. Woodson

Carter G. Woodson was born in Virginia in 1875 to a big family of former slaves. Carter grew up poor and could not regularly attend school. Back in those days, laws didn't protect children by requiring them to attend school. Instead, he had to work to support his family. Nevertheless, young Carter was very motivated, and taught himself every school subject.

As a young man, he earned a living mining coal and devoted all of his spare time to learning. He entered high school at the age of 20 and graduated in only two years. He became a teacher and later a principal at that same high school. While he worked, he took classes part-time and eventually completed his Ph.D. in history at Harvard University. He became the second African American, after W.E.B. Du Bois, to earn a doctorate. Then he became a professor at Howard University.

Through studying history, Carter found that the role of his own people and other minorities were being ignored or misrepresented among American history scholars. He realized the need to research the neglected history of Black Americans. So in 1915, he and some friends founded the Association for the Study of Negro Life and History. The following year, he began publishing a scholarly *Journal of Negro History*. In 2002 it was renamed the *Journal of African American History* and continues to be published. In all these years, the journal has never missed publishing an issue!

Carter believed that education and creating more social and professional contacts among Blacks and Whites could build bonds that would weaken racism. For that purpose, he promoted the first Negro History Week in Washington, D.C., in 1926. He chose a week celebrating the February birthdays of Frederick Douglass and Abraham Lincoln. This was the forerunner to Black History Month, of course!

So now you know why we celebrate Black History Month in February! It's because of the "Father of Black History," Carter G. Woodson!

Day 2 - Mo'Ne Davis

Mo'Ne Davis was born in 2001 in Philadelphia. She grew up going to a recreation center in her neighborhood to play football with her cousins and brother. One day one of the center's program directors saw Mo'Ne throw a football in perfect spirals and tackling kids who were bigger and stronger than she. Mo'Ne was playing football like a professional! When he saw how great of an athlete Mo'Ne was he asked her to come to basketball practice to watch. When Mo'Ne showed up she didn't want to watch; she wanted to play. After watching the practice she knew exactly what to do on the court. The director decided she needed to be on his basketball team. She agreed and became his best player and also the only girl on the team!

At the age of ten she was a point guard in basketball; a pitcher, shortstop and third baseman in baseball; and midfielder for soccer. Her favorite sport was basketball but it was her performance in baseball that landed her in the Little League World Series! This was a really big deal because there was a time when girls couldn't play Little League Baseball.

In 1972 a girl named **Maria Pepe** was the first girl to start in a Little League game, but she was removed when the other team didn't want to play against a girl. When The National Organization for Women filed a lawsuit for Maria Pepe, the judge ruled that the Little League Series had to let girls play. Decades later, Mo'Ne was the first girl in Little League World Series history to pitch a winning game and the first girl to pitch a shutout in Little League postseason history. She led her team to a 4-0 win and during the six innings she pitched, she struck out eight batters. That was the most watched Little League game on ESPN! So while Mo'Ne was not the first girl to start in a Little League game she was the very best!

She wrote a book about her life and designed a line of sneakers for girls. Now she is a philanthropist, supporting a charity to help millions of girls out of poverty worldwide. So the next time you want to do something that seems impossible, give it a try and be the very best you can be like Mo'Ne Davis!

Day 3 - Charlotte E. Ray

Charlotte E. Ray was born in 1850 in New York City, the youngest of three daughters. Her father was a minister, abolitionist and owner of a newspaper. Both of her parents valued learning and strove to provide their daughters with a proper education.

Little Charlotte moved with her family to Washington, D.C., where her parents sent her to the Institution for Colored Youth. This was the only local school that allowed African American girls to be students. When Charlotte graduated, she taught at Howard University, a historically Black college which was then only a few years old. She trained schoolteachers, but she really wanted to do something else with her career: practice law.

Two big obstacles stood in her way to become a lawyer: her race and her gender. But that didn't stop her! She applied to Howard University's Law School under the name "C.E. Ray" to disguise her gender. Her application was accepted and after it was discovered that she was a woman, officials at the university discouraged her from going through the program but allowed it nevertheless. Charlotte went through law school while continuing to teach her classes. She impressed her peers and teachers alike with her intelligence. In 1872 she completed law school and became the first Black woman with a law degree in the United States!

The bar in Washington, D.C. removed the word "male" from its requirements and Charlotte became the first woman admitted to it. She opened her law office there and skillfully argued many cases, earning the respect of many of her colleagues. But unfortunately, she experienced discrimination. Most people did not want to hire a Black woman attorney. Unable to make a living as a lawyer, she moved back to New York to live with her sisters and became a schoolteacher.

During her time in New York, she fought for women's suffrage and became a delegate to the 1876 conference for the National Women's Suffrage Association. Twenty years later, Charlotte joined the newly formed National Association of Colored Women.

Although she was only able to have a short career as a lawyer, she broke ground in a profession that had previously been reserved for White men. Her enormous achievement was unsung because she did not fully reap the benefits of her hard work in her lifetime. Today, many women are lawyers and have Charlotte E. Ray to thank for helping pave that road!

Day 4 - Josephine St. Pierre Ruffin

Josephine St. Pierre Ruffin was born in Boston in 1842 of mixed ancestry. She learned early on to fight against racial and gender discrimination. Josephine first attended segregated public schools, then her parents sent her to a private school in New York City, where she could get a good education regardless of her skin color. When segregation of schools ended in Boston, she returned home and finished her education there.

At the age of 16 she married George Ruffin, a young lawyer who was one of the first Blacks to graduate from Harvard Law School, and one of the first Black judges in the state. Together they became abolitionists. When the Civil War began they helped recruit Black soldiers for the Union Army and sent aid to Union soldiers. After they did their part to help Black people gain freedom, Josephine became especially interested in the rights of women. By joining several White groups that supported women's rights, Josephine gained organizational skills and influence in many integrated circles. She wrote articles about how women should be treated equally and became a journalist for a Black newspaper called *The Courant*. She also became a member of the New England Woman Press Association.

When George died in 1886, Josephine continued her social activism by starting the country's first newspaper published by and for Black women, called *Woman's Era*. The paper was very popular because it highlighted the achievements of Black women, and urged them to demand equal rights for all Blacks in America. Josephine formed numerous associations including the Women's Era Club, which supported the rights of Black women, and the Massachusetts School Suffrage Association. She tried many times to join other clubs for women in the South, but when they found out she and her club members were Black she was denied membership. Josephine never gave up the fight for equal rights. In 1910 she helped form the NAACP.

Women were finally given the right to vote in 1920 when the Nineteenth Amendment was passed thanks to the efforts of people like Josephine St. Pierre Ruffin. So at the next election, talk to a woman you know about voting and talk about Josephine St. Pierre Ruffin!

Day 5 - Henry "Box" Brown

Henry Brown was born a slave on a plantation in Virginia in 1815. When he grew up he married another slave and together they had four children. Sadly, his family was sold to another owner in North Carolina. Henry Brown's great loss moved him to silently vow to find a way to escape from slavery.

With the help of both Black and White friends from his church, he put a plan into action to mail himself to the North where he could be free! To get out of work for the day, he used sulfuric acid to burn his hand to the bone. His friend lined a crate with linen and cut a small hole in the top for air. Henry Brown climbed in the crate with a little bit of water and a few biscuits. His friend shipped the box from Richmond to Philadelphia, and Henry Brown's crate was moved by wagons, railroads, a steamboat, and a ferry. Finally, after 27 hours, it was delivered to his friends.

When his friends opened the box, Henry Brown grinned and exclaimed, "How do you do, gentlemen?" Then he recited a passage from the Bible, overjoyed at the great success of his plan. After his escape, abolitionist leaders couldn't agree on whether to share his strategy publicly. On one hand, some argued that going public with his method would make it harder for other slaves to escape this way. On the other hand, some thought that it would inspire other slaves to make clever and daring escapes too.

After much thought, Henry Brown decided to go public with his story. From that point on, he became known as Henry "Box" Brown. In the North, he developed a stage show called "Mirror of Slavery." His show gave him a platform to speak out against slavery to many people, first in the United States and later in England. Years later, he became a magician, and a part of his magic show involved the crate he used to escape!

Many people know about slaves escaping through the Underground Railroad, but few people know about Henry "Box" Brown's escape through the postal service. When you get a big box delivered in the mail, think about Henry "Box" Brown's great escape!

Day 6 - William Henry Cling

William Henry Cling was born in 1866 to former slaves in South Carolina. Life was hard for African Americans like William in the South, because they lived under unfair Jim Crow laws. But William overcame the hardships of growing up under such treatment!

When he grew up, he married and had six children. William became a barber who had a knack for thinking of great ideas and turning them into useful inventions. Interestingly, none of his inventions were related to his profession as a barber.

First he invented a mechanical device used to keep track of the number of people at a place. This invention, called the passenger register, was used especially at theatres or public events like fairs. It was a much better system than counting people and tallying with paper and pencil, like the previous system. A variation of these are still used today!

Nine years later, he invented a railway safety device to save people's lives! Frequently trains would have head-on or rear collisions if they were on the same track. He knew that there must be a way to fix this problem. So William set emergency brakes in the trains to prevent this.

Later he thought of an idea to put wires in shoelaces. With this new design, the laces could be tied with a simple twist. Last, he came up with a way to make life easier for people who were bed-ridden. He noticed that people who had to stay in bed because of injuries or sickness couldn't sit upright without great effort by their caretakers. So William designed a bed which could be folded into an upright position. These days, modern technology has improved these beds, and hospitals have them in every room!

Inventors make it their goal to make life easier. Think about ways to make life easier and turn those ideas into inventions! Then you will be like creative and clever William Henry Cling!

Day 7 - Matthew Henson

Matthew Henson was born in Southern Maryland in 1866. In order to escape harassment by groups like the Ku Klux Klan, his parents sold their farm and moved to Georgetown in Washington, D.C. His parents were poor but somehow Matthew knew he wanted to be an adventurer. At the age of 12, he worked as a cabin boy on a ship bound for China. He was promoted to seaman after one year, a promotion that usually takes four years!

At the age of 21 he met Robert Peary, who was then a naval lieutenant. He was so impressed with Matthew's knowledge of the sea that he made Matthew his personal attendant and they went on an expedition to Nicaragua. In 1891 Robert Peary started exploring the Arctic, and he took Matthew with him. They tried and tried but failed to make it all the way to the North Pole. The journey was really rough. It actually took them 18 years to finally to reach it. During their many expeditions, Matthew learned to communicate with the native people, the Inuit. He learned their language and how to drive dog sleds. Matthew was a skilled handyman who could solve many of the problems that came with traveling in the cold Arctic climate. He built igloos and made sure the expeditions were equipped with the right materials for clothing, food and supplies. He even made a dog sled that was better than the Inuit's, and it now sits in the American Museum of Natural History in New York.

In 1909 on their 8th attempt to reach the North Pole, the team covered thousands of miles and decided they needed to rest. While everyone slept, Matthew went out to explore more. When Robert Peary and the crew woke up, they went looking for Matthew. When they found him they took measurements and discovered that Matthew had been the first man to stand on the top of the world! When the team returned home no one really believed their story, especially since Matthew was a Black man. Robert Peary spent the next two years trying to prove his claim and the team was finally recognized as being the first to reach the North Pole.

Matthew wrote a book, *A Negro Explorer at the North Pole,* telling of his adventures. In 1944 Congress awarded him and five other Peary aides duplicates of the Peary Polar Expedition Medal. Presidents Truman and Eisenhower both honored Matthew before he died. Are you dreaming of a great adventure? Think about the experiences of Matthew Henson!

Day 8 – Susie King Taylor

Susan "Susie" King Taylor was born a slave in Georgia in 1848. She lived on a plantation until about the age of seven when she moved in with her grandmother, a free woman. Secretly, Susie was educated by both Black and White teachers who were willing to break the law to help. Her education ended when her grandmother was arrested for singing freedom hymns at church, and young Susie was forced to return to her mother on the plantation.

Then when she was 14, she and some family members took a risk and were able to escape from slavery during the Civil War. They got onto a gunboat and sailed to an island in Georgia that the Union Army held. There, Susie impressed the commanding officers with her ability to read and write, so they created a school for her to teach children and adults on the island. Susie became the first Black woman to teach in Georgia, and unlike her own education, she didn't have to do it secretly.

That same year Susie met Edward King, who was a Black officer in the 33rd United States Colored Infantry Regiment. They married and Susie began working as a nurse and doing the laundry for the troops, which made her the first Black Army nurse. She taught the soldiers how to read and write. In return the soldiers taught Susie a thing or two about guns and shooting. Susie moved to South Carolina and became a nurse at a hospital for Black soldiers. She ended up serving the Union Army for four years. Remarkably, she never received any pay for her work. Susie and Edward remained with the 33rd Regiment until they were discharged at the end of the Civil War.

Later, Susie wrote three books, including one that told of her Army experiences. Her publications made her the first and only Black woman to publish stories of her experiences as a nurse in the Civil War. Susie King Taylor had a passion for taking care of people. Will you do the same?

Day 9 - Alexander Miles

Alexander Miles was born in 1828 in Minnesota. He married, became a barber, and then he and his wife invested in real estate. Alexander purchased and operated a barber shop at the upscale St. Louis Hotel. He was successful in his business and became the first Black member of the Duluth Chamber of Commerce. In 1899 he sold his real estate investments in Duluth and moved to Chicago. There he founded The United Brotherhood, a life insurance company that would insure Black people who were often denied insurance coverage at that time. It was a very successful business because it helped many Black families financially.

One day while riding an elevator with his young daughter, Alexander saw that it was really dangerous when the elevator door was left open. In those days when an elevator would arrive at the selected floor, the outside door would open but the inside door of the shaft had to be opened and closed. An elevator operator or the passengers had to do this by hand. If someone was careless, the doors could be left open at any time, allowing someone to fall down the shaft. With this in mind, Alexander saw the need to design a mechanism that would automatically open and close elevator doors. He figured out how to attach a flexible belt to the cage. Then the elevator doors would automatically open and close at exactly the right time, and everything would be in synch. Once his invention was tested and proven to work Alexander applied for a patent, which was granted in 1887.

His invention to open and close elevator doors greatly improved elevator safety. So the next time you push the button for the elevator think about how Alexander Miles made them safe for you to ride.

Day 10 - George Washington Bush

George Washington Bush was born in Pennsylvania in 1789, the only child of his African father and Irish mother. When he grew up, he moved west and became a cattle rancher and fur trapper. Over time, George earned a small fortune and became known as one of the best fur trappers in Missouri. He wisely saved the money he earned from his trade.

In 1830 he married a nurse named Isabella James, and together they had nine sons! The Bush family and five other families decided to make a big move further west on the Oregon Trail. Back in those days, most of the people who lived in the Pacific Northwest were American Indians, and very few others made the dangerous trek west. The Oregon Trail was over 2,000 miles long, and groups traveled together in covered wagons. The Bushes bought covered wagons for the other five families to travel with them. Between his fur trapping, and her skills as a nurse, George and Isabella made a great team!

The Bush family history records that George built a false bottom into his covered wagon to hide silver and gold. Their original plan was to settle in present-day Oregon, but a new law did not allow Black people to own land there. Upon finding this out, the Bushes and their friends settled in present-day Washington in a territory that both the United States and Great Britain claimed.

Together they built a sawmill, a logging company and a farm. The Bushes built a hotel where anyone could stay for free. Weary travelers loved to stop there because the Bushes gave them a solid meal and crops grown on their farm. Together the Bushes helped their American Indian neighbors through epidemics of smallpox and measles. If a neighbor had a bad year with crops, George always shared happily, rather than selling his crops for a great profit.

Some historians say that George's generosity helped many Americans settle in Washington, which populated the territory. This helped settle the land dispute in favor of the United States. His influence in the Pacific Northwest was tremendous!

Undoubtedly, the Bushes were everyone's favorite neighbors. Whenever you have a chance to show kindness to your neighbors, take it and think about generous George Washington Bush!

Day 11 - Daniel Hale Williams

Daniel Hale Williams was born in 1856 in Pennsylvania. His family moved to Maryland and sadly, his father died when Daniel was a child. His mom decided she could not manage the entire family and sent some of the children to live with relatives. Daniel lived in many cities but ended up living in Wisconsin where he found work cleaning up and keeping things in order for a local physician, Dr. Henry Palmer.

He inspired Daniel to become a doctor, so he became an apprentice at Dr. Palmer's office. Daniel studied with Dr. Palmer for two years and then entered medical school in Chicago. He graduated and opened an office in 1883. He is hailed as the first Black cardiologist in the United States. As his medical and surgical practice grew, Daniel held various positions including an instructor position at Northwest University. He was one of only four Black doctors in the whole Chicago area, where his practice and reputation in the medical community grew. However, despite all his success, Black doctors were not permitted to work in most American hospitals. This disturbed him even more when he met a young Black woman who was refused admission to every nursing school in the area because of her race. Daniel decided there should be a Black owned hospital where young Black and White students could come to learn and provide excellent medical care for all. As a result he started Provident Hospital in 1891, the first non-segregated hospital in the United States.

One day in 1893 a man who was stabbed in the heart was rushed to Provident Hospital. It looked like there was nothing that could be done for him. Daniel thought more optimistically and decided to perform surgery. When he opened up the man's chest, Daniel found he had a pierced blood vessel and a tear to the area around the heart. Daniel repaired the damage, stopped the bleeding and the man lived for another 20 years! This surgery was the first successful open heart surgery ever performed. Daniel later went on to teach and create more hospitals for Black Americans.

So every time you hear your heart beat think about Dr. Daniel Hale Williams and how he "beat" the odds and performed a miracle!

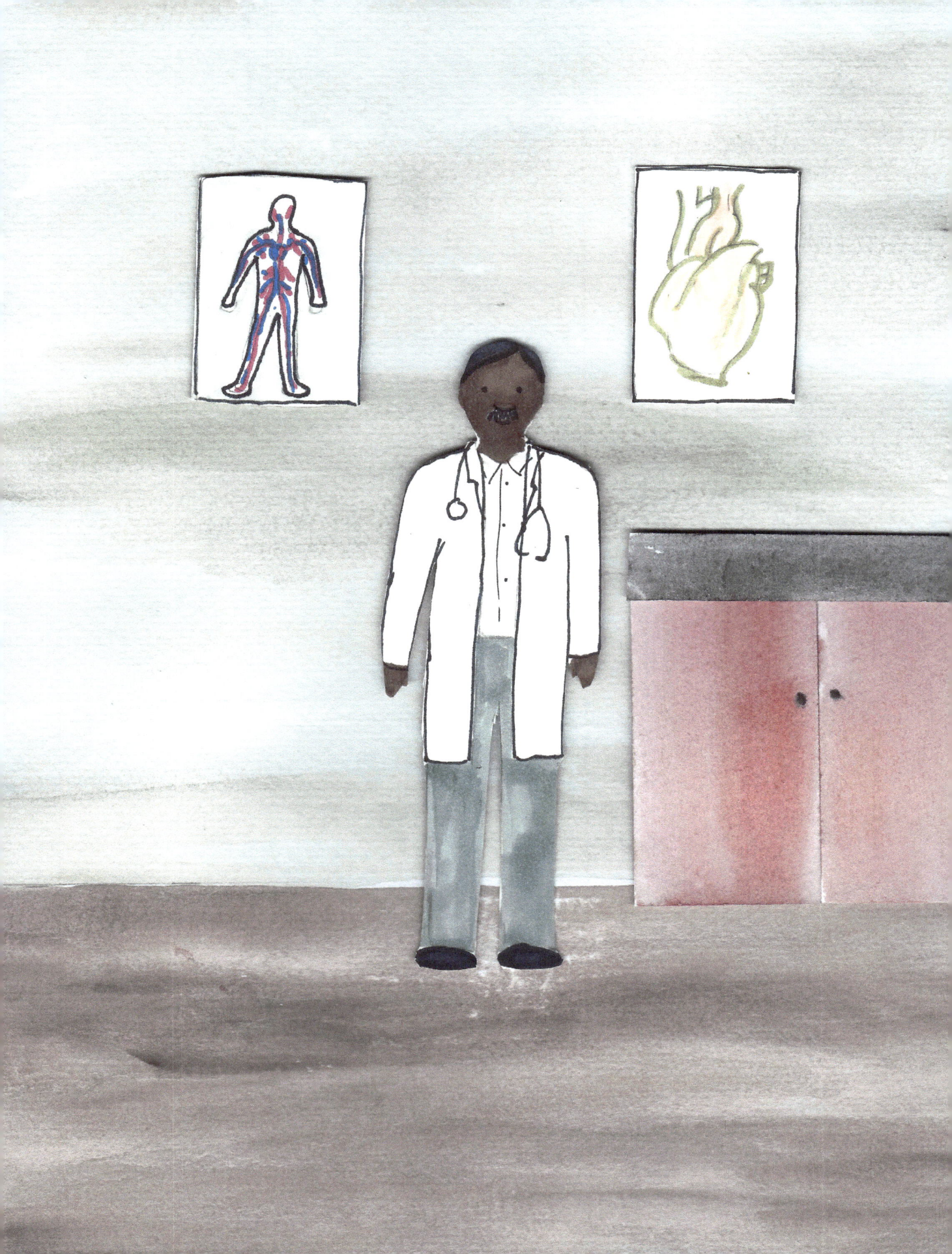

Day 12 - Elizabeth Taylor Greenfield

Elizabeth Taylor Greenfield was born a slave in Mississippi sometime between 1810 and 1820. Her childhood was quite different than most slaves. Elizabeth's owner, a widow named Holliday Greenfield, moved to Pennsylvania and took young Elizabeth with her. There, Mrs. Greenfield became a Quaker and freed her slaves in Mississippi. Although Elizabeth's parents moved to Liberia, Elizabeth continued to live with Holliday Greenfield and took her last name.

While living with her former owner, Elizabeth developed a love for music, playing the harp and piano at her church. But what she loved most was singing! She had a very rare talent to sing beautifully as a soprano, alto, tenor, and bass.

As a young woman, Elizabeth earned a living by singing publicly and got mixed reviews. On one hand, her talent was recognized by some newspapers that nicknamed her "African Nightingale" and "Black Swan." On the other hand, she dealt with racism, was denied proper vocal training, and got demeaning reviews from some other newspapers. Once she even performed under the threat of someone burning down the concert hall.

No one could stop her from singing though! Elizabeth became friends with Harriet Beecher Stowe, who helped her make connections to further her singing career. She received vocal training and had the great opportunity to perform around Europe. During this tour, Elizabeth sang at Buckingham Palace for Queen Victoria!

When she returned to the United States, she performed at charities benefitting Black Americans. She also trained other singers who would become legends like her. After she died, a record label took the name "Black Swan Records" in her honor. Whatever challenges you face, just keep singing your song, and you will be like Elizabeth Taylor Greenfield!

Day 13 - Benjamin Banneker

Benjamin Banneker was born 1731 in Ellicott's Mills, Maryland. He was said to be the son of freed slaves, and his mom was said to be a descendant of the African royalty of the Dogon people. They were widely known for their knowledge of astronomy, which is the study of stars and planets. Little Benjamin attended school and he taught himself many additional subjects that he found fascinating. A natural genius, he taught himself astronomy and successfully predicted lunar and solar eclipses.

In 1753 he created his own clock entirely of wood and it is famous for running for almost 50 years! Because Benjamin was so intelligent, the wealthy Ellicott family loaned him books on many subjects including astronomy and surveying land. Surveying land involves marking boundaries of land for buildings and cities. In 1791 one of the Ellicotts hired Benjamin to assist in surveying the land for what would be the capital of the United States, Washington, D.C. Benjamin was so smart he observed the stars and used his clock to give surveyors points to lay out the city. But he became sick so he couldn't complete the survey and had to return home.

Back home on his farm, Benjamin started to write and publish farmer's almanacs. These were handbooks of his own astronomical calculations that were helpful for farmers to know important things about the weather and when to plant crops. His writings included information on water tides to help fishermen, behavior of honey bees and the first calculations on the 17 year cycle of locusts. His almanacs became world-famous and he used his fame to promote social change. He spoke about how all people were brothers, why slavery needed to end, and why Black people should be given civil rights.

Benjamin was internationally known as a farmer, engineer, surveyor, city planner, astronomer, mathematician, inventor, author and critic of society. Next time you look at the stars think about how you too can be someone as smart as Benjamin Banneker and influence the world.

Day 14 - Annie Malone

Annie Malone was born between 1869 and 1877 in Illinois. Both parents died when she was very young so she was raised by an older sister. Annie grew to be a good student and studied hard, but she was a sickly child and missed a lot of school.

While home from school, Annie developed an interest in taking care of hair. She loved it so much she would practice on her sister. In those days many Black women used different kitchen ingredients like goose fat and bacon grease to make their hair less curly and more manageable. These oils damaged their hair and scalp and Annie wanted to solve this problem. So she talked to her aunt, an herbal doctor, and used her little knowledge of chemistry to experiment with different solutions. She was on a mission to create a hair straightener that wouldn't damage the hair or scalp. Finally she figured out a formula that worked so she developed and manufactured her own line of straighteners, oils and hair stimulants for Black women.

She moved to St. Louis where she had great success selling her product door to door. In 1914, Annie married Aaron Eugene Malone, a former teacher and religious book salesman. With his sales skills, he helped Annie open her own retail shop, manufacturing plant and beauty college. She trained women all over the United States to sell her products to gain their own financial independence. Her school was the first in the country dedicated to the study of Black cosmetology. It included teaching women on personal style, walking, talking and dressing properly in public.

Annie used her wealth wisely and was very generous to those in need. She gave away a lot of her money to colleges that accepted Black students and to the St. Louis Colored YWCA . She gave to the St. Louis Colored Orphans Home, which was later named the Annie Malone Children's Home in her honor and it still operates today! When you think of those in need, think of how Annie was a sick orphaned child but used her intelligence to create great products and help others. Will you do the same?

Day 15 - Jan Ernst Matzeliger

Jan Ernst Matzeliger was born in Guyana, South America in 1852. He was very skilled in mechanical things even as a child. At the age of ten he became an apprentice at a machine shop. When he finished his apprenticeship, he was eager to learn more and left Guyana to go to New York City. Even though he was at a disadvantage because he was Black and poor he was determined to learn more about machinery.

He left New York and moved to Massachusetts where he found a job operating a machine for turning shoes during the shoemaking process. He noticed that the process of "lasting" shoes wasted a lot of time. Shoe lasting is what makes the final shape of the shoe and holds it still so that the sole can be attached. Can you imagine making shoes by hand, holding the shoe shape upside down and nailing the sole to it? It was a very difficult and time consuming task! Shoe lasters were the most important workers in the shoemaking industry. They could turn out 50 pairs of shoes in a day. But because shoe lasters were so critical to the process they were bossy, and if they didn't want to come to work the factories had to shut down. Curious, he talked to some of his co-workers in the factory about making a machine for the process. Well, that was a shoemakers dream, but so far no one had succeeded in the invention.

With very little money, Jan gathered up as much material as he could find. He didn't want to be laughed at, so he worked in secret. Many others had tried to make a lasting machine and failed, and surely no one would believe a Black man could do it. He worked on his model for six years. He was very determined! Eventually his model was good enough to convince others to invest and he started a small company. Once he perfected his model he applied for a patent, which he received in 1883.

Experts today say there is no better method for fastening the upper shoe to the sole. With Jan's machine, a shoemaker could make 150 or more shoes in a day! Jan was able to get many patents for other shoemaking inventions and his machines are responsible for the increase and expansion of the shoe industry. So next time you put on your shoes, look at them closely and think about Jan Ernst Matzeliger!

Day 16 - Sophia Danenberg

Sophia Danenberg was born in Illinois in 1972 to a Japanese mother and Black father. As a girl, she was a great student and especially loved science. After high school, she studied environmental sciences and public policy at Harvard University. After she graduated, she went on to Keio University in Tokyo, Japan. She began her career managing energy and indoor air quality projects first in Asia, then in the United States.

After several years in a successful career, one of Sophia's friends encouraged her to try rock climbing and she found that she loved it! She began doing technical climbs at her local Appalachian Mountain Club Chapter, where she met her husband, David Danenberg. The two of them summited some of the world's most famous mountains together. Then she decided to tackle the biggest mountain in the world: Mount Everest. Located in Nepal, Mount Everest stands 29,000 feet high. When she decided to climb it, Sophia was in her mid-thirties and only trained for a few weeks to prepare for the treacherous hike. Most people hiking Mount Everest prepare for much longer since it is such a difficult climb.

She worked full-time while preparing and struggled purchasing equipment she needed. She wasn't able to find a down suit small enough for her, so she hiked in one way too big, and gave it away to a Sherpa friend at the hike's end. She did the hike unguided and made a lot of tough decisions on her own. On May 19, 2006, Sophia suffered from bronchitis, frostbite on her cheeks, a clogged oxygen mask, and she reached the top of Mount Everest nevertheless.

Sophia didn't know at the time of her hike that she was the first Black person to summit Mount Everest! She didn't do it to chase titles or fame, she simply loved to climb. In an interview after the hike, she noted the lack of diversity in the climbing community. She hopes to help change that!

Wherever you live, you can try taking hikes through the woods, mountains, or try a rock-climbing wall at a gym close to you. Then you can be like trailblazing Sophia Danenberg!

Day 17 - James McCune Smith

James McCune Smith was born a slave in 1813 in New York City. He had mixed ancestry and was raised by his mother. As a young teenager, he was freed when the state of New York made slavery illegal.

As a boy, James was exceptionally smart. After graduating from high school, he found that he would not be accepted at his local schools of choice because of his race. But that didn't stop James! He was accepted at the University of Glaslow in Scotland, and several of his high school teachers funded his trip and education overseas. He graduated at the top of his class with a medical degree.

When he returned to the United States, he married and had eleven children. He became a great success in his career as the first university-trained Black physician in the United States. He was also the first Black person to have articles published in American medical journals. During his 25 years practicing, he treated patients with diverse ethnic backgrounds. James also became the only doctor of the Colored Orphan Asylum, which kept him quite busy! He began a school and opened the first Black-owned pharmacy in the United States. The back room of the pharmacy became a meeting place for his Black and White abolitionist friends to work together.

His good friend Frederick Douglass described James as the single most influential person in his life! When abolitionist meetings would get heated and divisive, James was a peacemaker, calmly insisting on arguing from facts and analysis. Following this principle, James wrote a lot of articles for newspapers, and he was considered one of the great intellectuals of his time.

Perhaps one of the reasons that James is an unsung hero is because of poor record-keeping in his day. Historic documents often wrongly identified James as being White. For over a century, this wrong record remained uncorrected. But in recent years, his great-great-great granddaughter found his name in a family Bible, which led historians to properly identify James as being mixed race. His descendants gave him a new tombstone in 2010 which honored and correctly identified him.

So when you go to your local pharmacy, think about smart, level-headed James McCune Smith!

Day 18 - Emma Azalia Smith Hackley

Emma Azalia Smith Hackley was born in Tennessee in 1867 and loved music as a toddler. She became a child prodigy, which is a little kid who is extremely talented. She played piano at the age of three, and within a few years, she also became a gifted singer and violinist. Noticing her talent, many people suggested to her that she should claim to be White to help her advance her career. After all, she did have light skin and hair. But Emma would not deny her Black heritage and remained proud of her roots in spite of what others said.

She moved with her parents to Detroit, Michigan and graduated from high school. Then she became a schoolteacher and married Edwin Henry Hackley, a newspaper publisher and attorney from Colorado. Her husband's work inspired her, and she became an activist like him. Together they co-founded several organizations dedicated to helping Black Americans. She became the first Black person to graduate from the Denver School of Music in 1900.

Within a year, she devoted herself to a new mission in life - to educate African Americans in classical culture. Believing this would help lift them out of poverty, she described herself as a "race musical missionary." She traveled throughout the United States and held concerts singing "negro spirituals," training local performers to sing with her. Emma also gave local performers free classes on voice culture, and lessons on many other aspects of life. Through her classes, she emphasized the importance of being people of character.

She wrote books and articles on etiquette and her views that pride and self-help would lead to the racial uplift of Black Americans. Carry yourself with great dignity and be proud of your culture, just like Emma Azalia Smith Hackley.

Day 19 - Clara Brown

Clara Brown was born a slave in 1800 in Virginia. She was raised farming tobacco alongside her mother and other slaves. During her childhood, she and her mother moved with their owners to Kentucky.

There she married another slave, Richard, and together they had four children. Clara and Richard raised their children together for 17 years, and then their owner died. She and her family were sold at an auction, where they were all tragically separated from each other. Clara would never stop looking for her family.

Years later when Clara's second owner died, she was granted her freedom. She was 56 years old then, and slavery was still legal in the United States. There was a law that she couldn't live as a free woman in the state of Kentucky, so Clara moved west to Colorado. There, she worked several different jobs. Mostly she worked as a laundress, but she also was a skilled cook and midwife. Clara wisely invested the money she made from her jobs to buy land and gold mines in towns nearby. These investments made a lot of money for her! With her new wealth, she was generous. She opened up her home to the community, allowing it to be used as a church, hospital and home for the poor. Although she was unfairly discriminated against for the color of her skin, Clara joyfully served everyone, no matter their race. She used to say, "I always go where Jesus calls me." Clara became lovingly known as "Aunt Clara" because she took care of the needs of so many others.

When the Civil War ended, Clara was allowed to freely travel. So she sold everything she had to go back to Kentucky to search for her family. It took her many years, but finally when she was 82 years old, Clara Brown found one of her daughters, Eliza Jane. In the meantime, she paid the way for 16 other relatives and former slave friends to move to Colorado. She also helped a large group of freed slaves to build a community in Kansas. As an old lady, she was frail and had nearly run out of money from giving so much to so many. But Clara was rich where it counted! Her last years were filled with joy, as she spent them with her daughter, and devoted to God. During the last year of her life, she was voted into the Society of Colorado Pioneers, for her special role in the state's early history.

If you visit the beautiful state of Colorado, remember Clara Brown and all she did to help others!

Day 20 - Warren Shadd

Warren Shadd was born in 1956 in Washington, D.C. He was born into a very musical family that exposed him to jazz music. His mother was a great singer and his father was the number one piano technician for the Howard Theatre, where all the wonderful Black entertainers performed. As a child Warren could play the drums and had a talented ear for music. He was such an amazing drummer that he was hired to play his first concert at the age of four. Working at the theatre, his father became good friends with many famous performers of old jazz bands who would rehearse at the Shadd's house. Since Warren's father repaired pianos, you could count on pianos being all over the house; sometimes there wasn't enough space and pianos would even end up in the kitchen! Although his father encouraged Warren to learn to repair pianos, he just wanted to play the drums.

As he grew, Warren learned more about tuning and building pianos. Sometimes just for fun he would take an old piano apart and put it back together again, making it so perfect that his father would sell it. Throughout high school Warren continued to tour and play drums. Then he went on to Howard University, where he majored in music and played in a jazz band. They toured the world and recorded many albums. But Warren found that the road life of a musician was something he didn't really like. Then his father died in 1993, leaving his customers without help. Warren decided to take over the family business since he enjoyed tuning and repairing. Warren also created customized pianos. As a musician he had the advantage of knowing exactly what other musicians wanted to hear.

One day a customer gave him an idea to make his own pianos. So he studied some old manuals that explained how to enhance the sound of pianos. After a few experiments, Warren developed a piano that allows you to hear yourself play in real time, rather than hearing the aftereffect. He applied for several patents on his own unique piano technology, and his first patent was granted in 2003. He later built a model and put his name on it. Shadd Pianos became the first and only piano made by a Black man and the only musical instrument manufactured by a Black owned company. His pianos have appeared on television shows and are purchased by celebrities worldwide.

Now whenever you see a piano, check to see if it's a Shadd. If so, you know it's something very unique and special.

Day 21 - Elizabeth Jennings Graham

　　Elizabeth Jennings Graham was born sometime between 1826 and 1830 to a middle class family in New York. Her parents raised young Elizabeth to be involved in her church and Black community. Her father inspired her when he taught her about treating others fairly.

　　When she grew up, slavery was against the law in New York, but segregation was legal. There was an unfair law that Black passengers could ride streetcars as long as the White passengers on board said it was okay. One Sunday morning in the summer of 1854, Elizabeth and her friend got on a streetcar to go to church. The conductor told them to get off and she refused. He tried to remove her physically but she clung to the window. Finally, he called in a police officer and the two men pushed her off of the streetcar and into the street.

　　She was injured and outraged at the way she was treated. She boldly took some action, even though it seemed the law would be on the side of the conductor. First, she wrote a letter about her experience and sent it to her friends Frederick Douglass and Horace Greeley, who published it in the *New York Tribune*. Next, she and her friends held a rally to protest the violent way she had been treated. Last, she got a lawyer, the future President Chester Arthur, to sue the railway company. Against the odds, Elizabeth won the case! She was awarded money to pay for damages, which was a major victory for Black Americans! Even so, it still took 20 years to integrate streetcars in New York.

　　Most people know the story of Rosa Parks, who was arrested for a similar incident in 1955, but few people know the story of Elizabeth Jennings Graham, who took a stand on a streetcar a century earlier! The next time you sit on your school bus, sit where you want and think about brave Elizabeth Jennings Graham!

Day 22- Charlotte Forten

Charlotte Forten was born in 1837 in Pennsylvania to a wealthy and influential family. She grew up knowing friends of her parents, who were great intellectuals and politicians of her day. As a girl, she enjoyed writing and kept a diary. As it turned out, writing diaries was a wonderful habit for little Charlotte to form; as an adult, the diaries preserved her life work and now we know a lot about her thanks to them!

As a young woman, she was an abolitionist. Before the Civil War, she kept careful records of her daily work to end slavery. She became the first Black person hired to teach White students in Salem, Massachusetts. But after the Civil War began, she wanted to take part in something greater.

So she participated in the Port Royal Experiment, a movement committed to educating former slaves. Charlotte Forten moved to South Carolina during wartime to teach former slaves, giving them a chance for a good future. She recorded all of her amazing experiences in her diaries and essays. Her writings are a testament to her intellect, her culture, and her dedication. Charlotte Forten was determined to embody the great potential of all Black people. Below are a few of her diary entries and essays on teaching from her book *Life on the Sea Islands*.

"The long, dark night of the Past, with all its sorrows and its fears, was forgotten; and for the Future — the eyes of these freed children see no clouds in it. It is full of sunlight, they think, and they trust in it, perfectly."

"The first day of school was rather trying. Most of my children are very small, and consequently restless. But after some days of positive, though not severe, treatment, order was brought out of chaos. I never before saw children so eager to learn."

Charlotte Forten moved to Washington, D.C., married a minister later in her life and enjoyed a happy marriage. As an old lady, she was frail and suffered from health problems, but her dedication to social justice made her life fulfilling nevertheless.

Because she was first woman to do so many things, we call Charlotte Forten a pioneer! Maybe you will be a pioneer like Charlotte Forten!

Day 23 - William Carney

William Carney was born a slave in 1840 in Virginia. His father had escaped slavery through the Underground Railroad, then he worked until he was able to buy freedom for his wife and little William. After paying for their freedom, the Carney family moved to Massachusetts where young William was educated and dreamed of becoming a minister.

But the Civil War changed that dream for him. Instead he felt called by God to serve in the Union Army in the first all-Black Regiment. Because of his education and leadership skills, William quickly became a sergeant. His regiment first saw combat in South Carolina in 1863 when they charged Fort Wagner. The colonel and flag-bearer were mortally wounded in battle, and as William saw the American flag fall, he rushed to keep it from touching the ground. Though he was wounded in several places, he planted the flag in high ground during the heat of battle. Reinforcements arrived to withdraw the wounded troops and William carried the flag out. His heroism inspired his comrades to remain strong.

Proudly, he exclaimed, "Boys, the old flag never touched the ground!" Afterward, he was honorably discharged from the Army because of his wounds, but he remained an unsung hero for 37 years. All those years later William was awarded the highest military honor, the Congressional Medal of Honor. He was the first Black person to receive such an honor; previously it was given only to White men who showed bravery during battle.

After the Civil War ended, William married and had a daughter. He worked in civilian jobs and lived a happy life. He left behind a legacy of patriotism, in spite of the many challenges he faced as a Black American born into slavery. When you handle a flag, never let it touch the ground and think about patriotic William Carney!

Day 24 - Norbert Rillieux

Norbert Rillieux was born a free man in 1806 due to his privileged Creole family. His father was a prosperous engineer and inventor of the steam operated cotton baler. His mother was a slave. As a young child Norbert had all the education and privileges that slaves could not have. He was educated in schools in Paris where he studied engineering and became a teacher.

During this time in France, refining sugar was important to the economy. Refining sugar is making sugar cane into sugar crystals. It was a hard process that required lots of slaves in very dangerous situations. The slaves on sugar plantations had to transfer boiling hot cane liquid from one kettle to another, and the heat from the kettles couldn't be adjusted. Many slaves were severely burned and injured doing this work. Lots of sugar was lost in the transfer process because it would spill or get dropped from being too hot to handle. Norbert really wanted to solve the problem of how to take the moisture out of cane juice. This would make it safer for the slaves to carry and make a whiter, more refined crystal that would reduce waste and sell more sugar. It would be a new type of evaporation system.

Norbert's brothers and cousin in Louisiana began working to build a sugar refinery and asked Norbert to come and be their head engineer. Though they never finished the project, Norbert continued to develop and improve the evaporation system he was creating. He was able to complete an evaporation system that prevented spillage with an even spread of heat to keep the sugar from being burned and discolored. Once he received his patent for his method of industrial evaporation, he convinced many sugar factories to use his invention. This saved them lots of money and produced a better quality sugar. But even with all his success Norbert faced racial discrimination; he even had one of his patent applications rejected because they thought he was a slave and therefore not an American citizen.

In the 1850s, New Orleans suffered an outbreak of yellow fever. Norbert created a plan to use his evaporation system to drain the swamplands and improve the sewer system, keeping the insects from breeding and spreading the disease. The plan was rejected by Louisiana but later the state passed an almost identical plan presented by White engineers. Disgusted by so much racial prejudice, Norbert moved back to Paris and continued to invent more engineering systems. Next time you look at the sweet white sugar on your donut think about Norbert Rillieux!

Day 25 - Harriet Powers

Harriet Powers was born a slave on a Georgia plantation in 1837. It was on that plantation that many believe Harriet learned to sew, either from other slaves or from her lady owner. At a young age, she married Armstead Powers, a farmhand, and they had at least nine children.

After the Civil War, Harriet and Armstead became free and owned land in Georgia, but due to hard times they were forced to sell off part of their land. Eventually Armstead left the family, and Harriet began to take on sewing to earn money. It was just a matter of time before Harriet began making quilts.

The Bible and her own community became her inspiration to tell and share stories by sewing them onto the quilts. Many former slaves could not read or write, so creating pictures on quilts was a simple way to tell stories. Harriet became so well known for her story-telling quilts that she began to display them at cotton fairs. She hand and machine stitched them with small patches of cloth, colorful threads and designs.

At Harriet's first display, an artist named Jennie Smith saw the quilt Harriet called the Bible Quilt and offered to buy it. But Harriet refused to sell her prized possession. Jennie was fine with that and the two women stayed in touch with each other. As time passed Harriet had problems with money and finally agreed to sell Jennie her Bible Quilt for five dollars. But before Jennie would take the quilt away, Harriet made sure Jennie understood the stories sewn onto the quilt. Jennie wrote down every detail and put them in her personal diary.

The quilt had 299 separate pieces of fabric, made into 11 panels. The panels show pictures of Bible stories, like the story of Jacob climbing the ladder to heaven. This was a popular Bible story with slaves since they related to Jacob being hunted and homeless, and the ladder represented to them their eventual escape from slavery. Many believe that Harriet chose stories like these as secret messages of hope and escape. The Bible Quilt and one other remain to this day, and are on display at two museums.

Quilting was Harriet Powers' art. You can tell stories through your own kind of art too!

Day 26 - George Speck

George Speck was born in 1824 in Saratoga Lake in upstate New York. George took advantage of the mountain area of the Adirondacks, and for a while he worked as a mountain guide and animal trapper for fur.

In 1853 he got a job as a cook at a very expensive restaurant called Moon's Lake House. Because George was so skilled at cooking and creating recipes, he became the head chef. His sister Kate worked as a cook there too. One evening while cooking dinner, Kate was making french fries for a customer. The customer complained that they were too thick so he kept sending them back to the kitchen to be remade. George was not happy that someone complained about the food. So to get revenge he prepared one more batch of potatoes, but this time he sliced them super thin. He then fried them in oil, the same as the french fries, which made the potatoes dark and crisp. Determined to insult the customer, George added salt, put them on a plate and served them. But when the customer tried the thin crispy fries, he absolutely loved them!

From that point on George began preparing potatoes in this manner and they became known as "Saratoga chips." George's chips became so popular that people would come from all over just to get a taste. Some would even take the ten mile trip around the lake just to get to Moon's Lake House for his chips! The owner of the restaurant tried to take credit for creating the chips by producing and selling them in boxes with his name on them. Unfortunately, George never patented the potato chip so he never got credit for the invention. There is even speculation that the whole idea was actually his sister's.

In 1860 George decided it was time to open his own restaurant in Saratoga Lake. He named it Crums House, and he made sure to put potato chips as appetizers on every table. The restaurant was very successful and operated for 30 years. George never sold his chips other than in his restaurant.

Of course as we now know, potato chips are sold all over the world! So every time you eat a potato chip think about George Speck's success when he was just trying to teach a picky customer a lesson!

Day 27 - Ernest Green

Ernest Greene was born in 1941 in Little Rock, Arkansas. His family made sure that Ernest got a good education, and was active in his community, church and the Boy Scouts. He was a great kid and very well liked. When it was time for Ernest to attend high school, it was assumed he would go to the new high school that was assigned to the Black students. At that time most schools in the United States were segregated.

When Ernest entered high school 1954, the United States Supreme Court made a ruling that changed everything. The Brown vs. Board of Education case made segregation illegal. Even so, schools in the Southern states chose not to follow the new law. To help fight against this violation, the NAACP went to the state of Arkansas to see which schools would be the best for Black students to attend. They chose Central High School because it was a good school that was very close to where most of the Black students lived.

So Ernest Greene and eight other Black students volunteered to be the first to integrate the all-White Central High School in the fall of 1957. They were called the Little Rock Nine. Well, some of the people of Little Rock didn't like the idea of integration so they protested. On the first day of school they screamed at the Little Rock Nine and even tried to physically block them from entering the building. The governor sent the Arkansas National guard to support the White protesters, but President Dwight Eisenhower sent federal troops to protect Ernest and the other eight Black students. It was a very stressful year for the Black students. They were bullied and threatened many times, but they remained strong. They felt getting a fair and good education was worth it. Ernest was the only Black senior that year, which meant he had extra pressure on him to show everyone that Blacks could do well at Central High School and graduate like anyone else.

Ernest made history in 1958 when he became the first of the Little Rock Nine to graduate from Central High School. Martin Luther King, Jr. attended his graduation with Ernest's proud family. When you see something unfair speak out, and be brave like Ernest Greene!

Day 28 - Charlotte Hawkins Brown

Charlotte "Lottie" Hawkins Brown was born in 1883 in North Carolina, the granddaughter of a slave. When Lottie was born Jim Crow laws made life difficult for Black Americans living in the South. At the age of seven, she moved north to Massachusetts, and as she grew to be a teenager, she was self-disciplined to learn all she could and earn money babysitting. Lottie recalled pushing a baby in a stroller while reading aloud from a Latin book when her life changed for better. A woman named Alice Freeman Palmer, the president of Wellesley College, overheard her reading and decided at that moment to become her mentor and help Lottie further her education.

Lottie moved back to North Carolina where she taught in a small town school which closed after her first year for lack of funds. Determined to fix the problem, Lottie began to raise funds for the school, asking her mentor for financial aid. Her campaigns were successful; the next year Lottie opened a new school in the same small town called Palmer Memorial Institute, which she named after her mentor. The school earned a reputation for excellence, and during her time teaching there, Lottie had the honor of meeting some other great teachers of her day - Mary McLeod Bethune, Booker T. Washington, and Eleanor Roosevelt. Her school expanded to include a junior college program.

By 1920, Lottie was a well-known public figure and was in high demand as a speaker. She spoke against Jim Crow laws and on the value of education, on race, on women's rights, and even on social graces. She was the author of several books on these topics too. She urged her students to act with kindness and dignity, believing this would speed up the long and hard process of earning equal rights. Think about the great privilege it is to have an education and make much of it, just like Charlotte Hawkins Brown!

Day 29 - Bonus!

This is an excerpt from a book written by Charlotte Hawkins Brown on classroom etiquette:

The Classroom

1. Always greet the teacher when meeting for the first time, whether it be morning or not.
2. Be sure that you have everything you need - text, paper, pen, etc. Don't be a carpenter without tools.
3. When called on to recite, always make some sort of reply. Don't sit in the seat and say nothing. Don't even think too long. Valuable minutes are wasted thus.
4. When standing or sitting, hold yourself erect. Don't slouch. Talk clearly and sufficiently loud for everyone in the room to hear.
5. Don't make a habit of laughing at the mistakes of others. This often hinders a person from doing his best.
6. Don't deface property. Writing on or cutting into desks or chairs, writing and drawing in books, breaking the backs, or turning down the corners of pages of texts are evidences of poor training.
7. Make it your business to keep the room in order. Straighten the shades, keep the floor and desks free of waste paper, and erase the boards when they need it.
8. Don't Cheat. You will never learn by "copying" from your neighbor or from the book.
9. Do not argue with or contradict the teacher in class. If you think that she has made a mistake, wait until the hour is over and discuss it with her quietly at the desk.
10. Do not yell out the answers to questions; wait until you are called upon. The teacher will let you know when concert recitation is desired.
11. Don't mistake the classroom for a lunchroom or a bedroom.

Consider all of the heroes in this book. They accomplished great things by learning all that they could and doing much with what they learned. So when you go to class, follow the rules of etiquette laid out by Lottie Hawkins Brown and you will be a great success!

Bibliography

"A Student Remembers." *Charlotte Hawkins Brown Museum.* North Carolina Historic Sites. 06 Oct. 2015. Web. 07 Aug. 2018.

African American Registry.org editors. "Josephine Ruffin, activist, philanthropist, and newspaper publisher." *AAREG.* Web. 04 Jan. 2019.

Biography.com Editors. "Henry "Box" Brown Biography." The Biography.com website. A&E Television Networks. 22 Aug. 2019. Web. 11 Jan. 2020.

BlackInventor.com editors. "George Crum: Inventor of Potato Chips." *BlackInventors.com.* Famous Black Inventors: A Rich Heritage Gives Way to Modern Ingenuity. Web. 09 Jan. 2019.

Biography.com editors. "Charlotte Hawkins Brown Biography." *The Biography.com website.* A&E Television Networks. 26 Sep. 2015. Web. 07 Aug. 2018.

Biography.com editors. "Clara Brown Biography." *The Biography.com website.* A&E Television Networks. 21 Sep. 2015. Web. 24 Jun. 2018

Biography.com editors. "Charlotte Forten Biography." *The Biography.com website.* A&E Television Networks. 01 Apr. 2014. Web. 10 Aug. 2018.

Biography.com editors. "Elizabeth Jennings Graham Biography." *The Biography.com website.* A&E Television Networks. 20 Oct. 2015. Web. 16 Aug. 2018.

Biography.com editors. "Elizabeth Taylor Greenfield Biography." *The Biography.com website.* A&E Television Networks. 01 Apr. 2014. Web. 09 Sep. 2018.

Biography.com editors. "Matthew Henson Biography." *The Biography.com website*. A&E Television Networks. 02 Apr. 2014. Web. 12 Dec. 2018.

Brenton, Felix. "Danenberg, Sophia (1972-). *BlackPast.org.* Remembered & Reclaimed. Web. 29 Dec. 2018.

Cabiao, Howard. "Ray, Charlotte E." *BlackPast.org.* Remembered and Reclaimed. 2017. Web. 12 Aug. 2018

"Harriet Powers (1837-1911)." *americanartgallery.org.* Web. 14 Jan. 2020.

Helm, Matt. "Carney, William H. (1840-1908)." *BlackPast.org.* Remembered and Reclaimed. 2017. Web. 26 Sep. 2018

Jenkins, Willard. "The First African-American Piano Manufacturer." *A Blog Supreme from NPR Jazz*. National Public Radio. 07 May 2014. Web. 13 Jan. 2019.

"Madame Emma Azalia Smith Hackley." *Historic Elmwood Cemetery & Foundation.* Where Detroit's History Endures. Web. 15 Oct. 2018

McHugh, Catherine. "Who Was Charlotte E. Ray?" *The Biography.com website*. A&E Television Networks. 21 Sep. 2015. Web. 24 Jun. 2018.

Mitchell, Adam. "Conversation with Sophia Danenberg: First African American to Climb Everest." *Melanin Base Camp*. 31 Jan. 2018. Web. 29 Dec. 2018.

MyBlackHistory.net editors. "Alexander Miles." *MyBlackHistory.net.* Web. 14 Dec. 2018.

MyBlackHistory.net editors. "Norbert Rillieux." *MyBlackHistory.net.* Web. 14 Dec. 2018.

MyBlackHistory.net editors. "Daniel Hale Williams." *MyBlackHistory.net.* Web. 14 Dec. 2018.

Olsen, Winnifred and Shanna Stevenson. "George Bush (1789?-1863)." blackpast.org. 19 Jan. 2007. Web. 3 Dec. 2019.

"Only a Teacher: Charlotte Forten." *PBS.org,* WETA. Web. 10 Aug. 2018

Peterson, Heather. "Hackley, Emma Azalia (1867-1922)." *BlackPast.org.* Remembered and Reclaimed. Web. 15 Oct. 2018.

Rogers, J.A. *World's Great Men of Color, Volume II.* Macmillan Publishing, 1972.

"Susie Baker King Taylor." *Battlefields.org.* American Battlefield Trust. Web. 14 Jan. 2020.

"Susie King Taylor." *nps.gov.* National Park Service. 30 Mar. 2019. Web. 14 Jan. 2020.

"Warren M. Shadd: About." ShaddPianos.com. Web. 13 Jan. 2019.

Wikipedia contributors. "Benjamin Banneker." *Wikipedia, The Free Encyclopedia.* Wikipedia, The Free Encyclopedia, 12 Dec. 2018. Web. 13 Dec. 2018.

Wikipedia contributors. "Clara Brown." *Wikipedia, The Free Encyclopedia.* Wikipedia, The Free Encyclopedia, 8 May. 2018. Web. 24 Jun. 2018.

Wikipedia contributors. "Henry Box Brown." *Wikipedia, The Free Encyclopedia.* Wikipedia, The Free Encyclopedia, 8 Jan. 2020. Web. 11 Jan. 2020.

Wikipedia contributors. "George Washington Bush." *Wikipedia, The Free Encyclopedia.* Wikipedia, The Free Encyclopedia, 14 Nov. 2019. Web. 1 Dec. 2019.

Wikipedia contributors. "William Harvey Carney." *Wikipedia, The Free Encyclopedia.* Wikipedia, The Free Encyclopedia, 6 Sep. 2018. Web. 27 Sep. 2018.

Wikipedia contributors. "William Henry Cling." *Wikipedia, The Free Encyclopedia.* Wikipedia, The Free Encyclopedia, 18 Oct. 2017. Web. 24 Sep. 2018

Wikipedia contributors. "George Crum." *Wikipedia, The Free Encyclopedia.* Wikipedia, The Free Encyclopedia, 9 Jan. 2019. Web. 9 Jan. 2019.

Wikipedia contributors. "Sophia Danenberg." *Wikipedia, The Free Encyclopedia.* Wikipedia, The Free Encyclopedia, 22 Dec. 2017. Web. 29 Dec. 2018.

Wikipedia contributors. "Mo'ne Davis." *Wikipedia, The Free Encyclopedia.* Wikipedia, The Free Encyclopedia, 22 Nov. 2018. Web. 10 Jan. 2019."

Wikipedia contributors. "Ernest Green." *Wikipedia, The Free Encyclopedia.* Wikipedia, The Free Encyclopedia, 13 Jan. 2019. Web. 14 Jan. 2019.

Wikipedia contributors. "Emma Azalia Hackley." *Wikipedia, The Free Encyclopedia*. Wikipedia, The Free Encyclopedia, 18 Jan. 2018. Web. 15 Oct. 2018.

Wikipedia contributors. "Matthew Henson." *Wikipedia, The Free Encyclopedia*. Wikipedia, The Free Encyclopedia, 29 Nov. 2018. Web. 13 Dec. 2018.

Wikipedia contributors. "Annie Malone." *Wikipedia, The Free Encyclopedia*. Wikipedia, The Free Encyclopedia, 30 Nov. 2018. Web. 13 Dec. 2018.

Wikipedia contributors. "Jan Ernst Matzeliger." *Wikipedia, The Free Encyclopedia*. Wikipedia, The Free Encyclopedia, 4 Dec. 2018. Web. 7 Dec. 2018.

Wikipedia contributors. "Harriet Powers." *Wikipedia, The Free Encyclopedia*. Wikipedia, The Free Encyclopedia, 9 Jan. 2020. Web. 14 Jan. 2020.

Wikipedia contributors. "James McCune Smith." *Wikipedia, The Free Encyclopedia*. Wikipedia, The Free Encyclopedia, 1 Dec. 2018. Web. 6 Dec. 2018.

Wikipedia contributors. "Susie Taylor." *Wikipedia, The Free Encyclopedia*. Wikipedia, The Free Encyclopedia, 21 Oct. 2019. Web. 14 Jan. 2020.

Wikipedia contributors. "Norbert Rillieux." *Wikipedia, The Free Encyclopedia*. Wikipedia, The Free Encyclopedia, 22 Jun. 2018. Web. 16 Dec. 2018.

Wikipedia contributors. "Josephine St. Pierre Ruffin." *Wikipedia, The Free Encyclopedia*. Wikipedia, The Free Encyclopedia, 22 Nov. 2018. Web. 4 Jan. 2019

Wikipedia contributors. "Madam C. J. Walker." *Wikipedia, The Free Encyclopedia*. Wikipedia, The Free Encyclopedia, 23 Dec. 2018. Web. 4 Jan. 2019.

Wikipedia contributors. "Daniel Hale Williams." *Wikipedia, The Free Encyclopedia*. Wikipedia, The Free Encyclopedia, 13 Nov. 2018. Web. 16 Dec. 2018.

Wikipedia contributors. "Carter G. Woodson." *Wikipedia, The Free Encyclopedia*. Wikipedia, The Free Encyclopedia, 2 Jan. 2019. Web. 7 Jan. 2019.

Winter, Kari J. "Smith, James McCune (1813-1865)." *BlackPast.org* Remembered & Reclaimed. 2017. Web. 5 Dec. 2018.

www.ingramcontent.com/pod-product-compliance
Lightning Source LLC
Chambersburg PA
CBHW060819090426
42738CB00002B/44